Steamboats

The Story of Lakers, Ferries, and Majestic Paddle-Wheelers

Karl Zimmermann

Photography by the author

BOYDS MILLS PRESS

HONESDALE, PENNSYLVANIA

For Lily, as she sets sail

Acknowledgments

Special thanks to Conrad Milster, a noted authority on steam power and propulsion, for help with technical details.

Thanks also to Lucette Brehm of the Delta Queen Steamboat Company for assistance in gathering materials and information.

I am grateful for permission to use photographs from these archives:

The Steamship Historical Society
   of America Collections (pp. 12 and 13).
The Collection of the Public Library of
   Cincinnati and Hamilton County (p. 16).
The Historical Collections of the Great
   Lakes, Bowling Green State University (p. 36).

—K. Z.

Boyds Mills Press, Inc.
A Highlights Company
815 Church Street
Honesdale, Pennsylvania 18431
Printed in China
www.boydsmillspress.com

Library of Congress Cataloging-in-Publication Data

Zimmermann, Karl R.
  Steamboats : the story of lakers, ferries, and majestic paddle-wheelers / by
Karl Zimmermann ; photography by the author.
    p. cm.
ISBN-13: 978-1-59078-434-1 (hardcover : alk. paper)
1. Lake steamers—Juvenile literature. 2. River steamers—Juvenile literature.
3. Paddle steamers—Juvenile literature. 4. Ferries—Juvenile literature. I. Title.

VM460.Z55 2006
623.82'436—dc22

       2006018270

First edition, 2007
The text of this book is set in 13-point Minion.

10 9 8 7 6 5 4 3 2 1

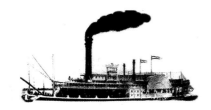

Contents

Introduction
Steaming Across the Great Lakes 5

One
Steam Takes Over 11

Two
Mississippi River Steamboating 15

Three
Excursion Steamers for Day-Trippers 23

Four
Ferryboats, Workhorses of the Water 29

Five
Bulk Carriers Serve the Great Lakes 33

Six
Trains Across the Water 39

Seven
Keeping Steam Up 45

Author's Note 47

Glossary 47

Index 48

Wheelsman at the helm of cement carrier S. T. Crapo.

Introduction

Steaming Across
the Great Lakes

IN THE LATE YEARS OF THE TWENTIETH CENTURY, an old-fashioned boat took me on a trip around the Great Lakes. Toting cement, this vessel had the unmistakable and unique look of a "laker," a bulk carrier built to haul iron ore, coal, grain, cement, and other commodities. Long and low, such lake boats have a forward wheelhouse, where captain and mates navigate, and a smokestack-topped "aftercabin." In between stretches a series of cargo holds nearly the length of a football field.

If the shape of this vessel was traditional, what went on inside its hull was even more so. This laker was not only powered by steam, a dying technology, but it had the very type of propulsion that had begun driving boats across water two centuries earlier—a reciprocating engine. On the Great Lakes, such reciprocating steamers are called "up-and-downers" because they are powered by the thrust of vertical pistons turning a crankshaft—in contrast to the whirling steam turbines that were developed much later and remain in occasional use today.

Just being a reciprocating steamer would have made this boat—the *S. T. Crapo*, built in 1927—obsolete by the time I boarded at

◄ *The S. T. Crapo is buffeted by high winds in this view from the wheelhouse looking back across the cement holds toward the aftercabin.*

■ 5

Alpena, Michigan. Even more remarkable was the fact that its boilers were fired by coal, when for many years most steamboats had burned oil. When I climbed up a rope ladder and onto the steamer's broad deck, I was also stepping into a world of yesterday's technology.

It was a gray morning in very late October, so we weren't too far away from the "gales of November," the stormy period that proved fatal to the lake boat made famous by singer-songwriter Gordon Lightfoot in "The Wreck of the *Edmund Fitzgerald*." The Great Lakes—Ontario, Erie, Huron, Michigan, and Superior, which together hold half of the world's fresh water—are big, imposing, potentially perilous inland oceans.

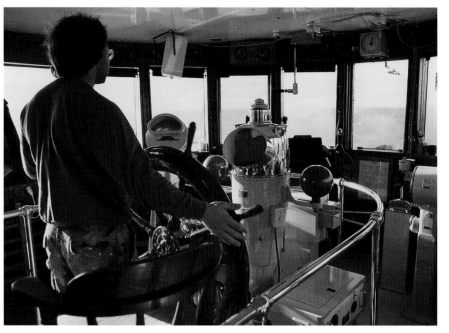

Lake Huron gleams through the arc of windows in the S. T. Crapo's wheelhouse. Storm clouds lie ahead.

Right from the beginning of my trip, the *Crapo*'s young master, Captain John Basel, was concerned about the weather, which was already blowing up.

Captain John Basel has rung down "full ahead" on the "telegraph" to the engine room, and the S. T. Crapo *is steaming along at 12 miles an hour.*

The S. T. Crapo Sets Sail

In charge in the vessel's old-fashioned, brass-ornamented wheelhouse, Basel rang down a "slow astern" to the engine room on the electric "telegraph." Deep in the bowels of the boat, Chief Engineer Dwayne Hunt rang back an acknowledgment. He opened the throttle, and the big engine lumbered into motion. Once Roger Kelly, the wheelsman whose bandanna and drooping mustache had earned him the nickname "Pirate," had pointed the *Crapo* toward the channel, Basel rang down a "full ahead."

The tension in the wheelhouse eased, but not for long,

since the weather worsened as we headed north. The routine four-day voyage to drop cargo at St. Joseph and Waukegan on opposite shores of Lake Michigan obviously wasn't going to happen as planned. By nightfall, the front edge of a squall hit, and the wheelhouse was alive with vibration from the wind, moaning and shrieking. Then suddenly it stopped, and everything became eerily still. By morning, however, the weather had gotten even worse.

"We're at a place called Death's Door," Sam Rogers told me. Sam was third mate—and, for me, roommate, as I was sharing his cabin. It was his watch. I looked at the chart and found Porte des Morts Passage, meaning "Death's Door," named by the region's French explorers in the seventeenth century.

The S. T. Crapo *waits out the storm in Milwaukee.*

Wearing a hat and gloves against the heat, a fireman rakes out the clinkers in the stokehold.

Rocky shores and strong winds and currents make this a dangerous passage and site of many shipwrecks.

"Mark," Sam said to the watchman on duty, "be sure the Use the Tunnel sign is up, and throw salt anywhere you see icing." A tunnel below deck connected the wheelhouse and aftercabin. In good weather the crew would go back and forth between the two by walking on deck, but on a day like this, that would have been unsafe. Then Sam explained our change in plans.

"Since it's on the east side of Lake Michigan, St. Joseph is exposed to these northwest winds," he said, "so we'll slip down to Milwaukee, sailing close to the west shore for shelter— 'beachcombing' we call it—and tie up until the wind drops."

Meanwhile, down in the stokehold, the area deep in the hull with fireboxes and coal bunkers, fireman "Bluewater" Bill Corell plied his hot, sooty, smoky trade, operating the mechanical stoker and cleaning the fires with a long-handled rake, pulling out the burned "clinkers" in a fiery cascade of hot coals. Ash flew everywhere, and pungent coal smoke hung in the air. Actually, Corell and the two other firemen who shared his job in shifts had it relatively easy. Before the installation of automatic stokers in 1962, they would have had to shovel the coal into the six fireboxes by hand.

The engine room was adjacent to the stokehold. Later, with the *Crapo* approaching the breakwater in Milwaukee in the wee hours of the morning, the alarm there squawked loudly enough to be heard over the engines' clamor, calling Third Assistant Engineer Gilmore to the telephone. The rollicking song of pistons slowed as Gilmore throttled down to "half

ahead" at the captain's request, then "slow," then "dead slow." Finally, once the boat was snugly alongside the pier in the sheltered harbor, Basel rang down "finished with engines" and my trip was over. The *Crapo* would be hunkered down there for days, waiting out the weather, and I couldn't wait with it.

Voyages Ahead

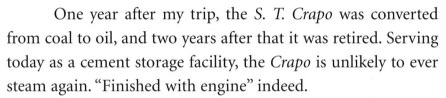

One year after my trip, the *S. T. Crapo* was converted from coal to oil, and two years after that it was retired. Serving today as a cement storage facility, the *Crapo* is unlikely to ever steam again. "Finished with engine" indeed.

But as I disembarked, I knew that I would board other steamboats. Paddle-wheelers dot the lakes of Switzerland, and I've tracked them down. The famous *Delta Queen*, built in 1927, the same year as the *Crapo*, sails the Mississippi, Ohio, and other inland rivers, as do her younger sisters *Mississippi Queen* and *American Queen*. I would experience all three. Trim little steam excursion boats flit among the islands off Stockholm, Sweden. The *Segwun* steams across the Muskoka Lakes in Ontario. The former railroad car ferry *Badger* crosses Lake Michigan. I've come to know them all.

Happily, many opportunities remain for me to sail with the breeze in my face and the throb of a reciprocating steam engine underfoot; to watch the splash of a paddle wheel or the churn of a propeller-generated wake; to see pistons flail and connecting rods dance; and to hear the throaty call of a steam whistle and the trill of an engine-room telegraph as the captain rings down "full ahead!"

The engine room.

One

Steam Takes Over

THROUGH THE NINETEENTH CENTURY, STEAMBOATS and steamships changed water transport in much the same way that steam locomotives transformed land travel. Before steam, sail power ruled the oceans, lakes, and larger rivers of the world. On canals, plodding mules and horses pulled barges cross-country at a snail's pace. On some rivers, goods and commodities were rafted downstream, with the boxy, bargelike flatboats themselves becoming a commodity when, at the end of their journeys, they were broken up and their wood sold for lumber.

Beginning in the early 1800s, the Age of Steam changed all that. At first, steam engines were used together with sails, one form of power supporting the other. Soon, however, as the steam plants became more powerful and reliable, the sails were eliminated. On excursion steamers the public traveled for fun, and on overnight "packets" for transportation. (A packet was a boat that carried passengers, freight, and mail on a set schedule over a short route.)

Steam was first used to power paddle wheels—sometimes affixed to the vessels' sides and sometimes at the stern, or back. Propellers were the next development, though some side-wheelers and stern-wheelers were built through the middle of the twentieth century. On the high seas and, much later, the Great Lakes, steam turbines

◀ *Though built in 1902, the graceful* Unterwalden, *which still sails on Switzerland's Lake Luzern, has much in common with the earliest steamboats.*

largely replaced reciprocating steam engines. Elsewhere, however, most steamboats were always powered by reciprocating, piston-driven engines.

The distinction between the general terms "boat" and "ship" is much debated. The definitions of "steamboat" and "steamship" are relatively straightforward, however. Steamboats ply inland lakes (including the vast Great Lakes), rivers, and coastal waters. Steamships, which were developed slightly later, sail the high seas.

The Age of Steam Begins

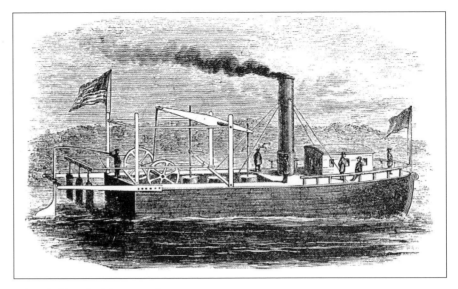

John Fitch's primitive steamboat.

The Age of Steam can be dated from 1712, almost a century before the first successful steamboat, when Thomas Newcomen installed a cumbersome stationary steam engine to pump water from a coal mine in England. In 1769, James Watt, a Scotsman, patented a dramatically improved engine, but one still too large to power boats or trains. For a stationary engine, great size and weight were not particularly a problem, except when they increased construction costs. On a boat or locomotive, however, size and weight became critical factors, as the engine of course had to be carried along for the ride.

Though steam locomotives and railroads lay half a century in the future, inventors almost immediately began to ponder how steam power might be used to move boats across the water. Sails worked, but they needed the cooperation of the winds, while steam would be consistently reliable.

The first American steamboat, a 45-foot-long experimental vessel built by New Englander John Fitch, crossed the Delaware River in August 1787, powered by oarlike paddles that emulated an Indian war canoe. Fitch built three additional boats, replacing that propulsion arrangement with a paddle

wheel centrally located within the hull. The public never thought of the boats as more than novelties, however. Fitch gave up and shut down the operation.

This opened the way for Robert Fulton to become the generally acknowledged "father of steamboating." He figured out how to make steamboats economical and, in so doing, kicked off a long-lasting run of paddle-wheel steamers on the Hudson River. This period ended in 1971, when the *Alexander Hamilton*, built in 1924 and the last of the Hudson River Day Line steamers, was retired.

For many years the Day Line, founded in 1863, had a nocturnal counterpart, the Hudson River Night Line, which ran overnight service between New York City and Albany. Since the Night Line was selling transportation, not recreation, it could not compete with the railroads, which ran up both banks of the Hudson. Thus, the Night Line shut down in 1939.

Its rise and fall paralleled that of steamboat lines all around the world: growth through the nineteenth century and into the early years of the twentieth, then slow, progressive demise. By 1950, survivors were few.

Robert Fulton and the Clermont

Robert Fulton didn't invent the steamboat, though many people think he did. He was, however, the first person to make a commercial success of steamboat operations. Most histories record his first vessel as the *Clermont*, and that's technically inaccurate, too.

A Pennsylvanian born in 1765, Fulton was an artist turned engineer and inventor, working in Great Britain and then in France. There he met Robert R. Livingston, who would be his partner in steamboat ventures to come. Of a wealthy and politically connected New York State family, Livingston (who helped draft the Declaration of Independence) would provide funds and influence. Fulton provided the know-how.

Though their first steamboat, launched in 1803 on the Seine, in Paris, would sink, they'd have much better success back in the United States. Livingston had secured a monopoly from the New York State Legislature on steamboat operations throughout the state. The most promising route was the roughly 150 miles of the Hudson River from New York City to Albany, the state capital. There, on August 17, 1807, Fulton's vessel made its first, experimental journey. Powered by paddle wheels with a modest assist from sails, it was called simply *North River Steam Boat*, a name it would retain until it was retired in 1814, the year before Fulton's death. ("North River" is another name for the Hudson River, used particularly by mariners.)

Though the vessel entered commercial service immediately, it was slightly enlarged and improved during its first winter lay-up. (Because of ice and, in the case of excursion boats, weather that was too cold for recreation, steamboats often went out of service in the winter.) When it was reregistered, by Livingston, it was as the *North River Steam Boat of Clermont*. (Clermont was his family estate on the Hudson.) An early biographer called the boat *Clermont*, and that's how it's been known since.

Steamboats would thrive on the Hudson River for more than a century and a half, but Fulton and Livingston knew there were great opportunities elsewhere, too—particularly in the West, where expansion and development were just beginning. With a partner, they constructed a shipyard in Pittsburgh, Pennsylvania, which built the first steamboat to ply the inland rivers. Called the *New Orleans*, the vessel sailed for its namesake city in September 1811, opening a long and illustrious history of Ohio and Mississippi river steamboat operations.

This replica of Robert Fulton's famous North River Steam Boat *was built in 1909 for the Hudson-Fulton Celebration, marking the three hundreth anniversary of Hudson's "discovery" of the river and (two years late) the one hundreth anniversary of the boat's launching.*

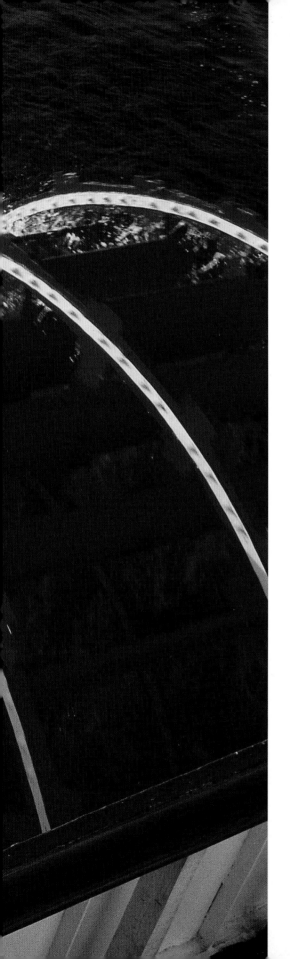

Two

Mississippi River Steamboating

THOUGH THE HUDSON RIVER WAS HOME TO THE FIRST commercially successful steamboat in the United States, the Mississippi is probably the river richest in steamboat history. It was, and remains, a huge artery for shipping that reaches deep into the heart of Middle America. The Mississippi itself is navigable for 1,793 miles, all the way from Minnesota's "Twin Cities," St. Paul and Minneapolis, to the Delta, where it flows into the Gulf of Mexico. No less important is the Ohio River, which joins the Mississippi at Cairo, Illinois. From there, steamboats churned 982 miles upstream to Pittsburgh, where the Ohio is formed when the Allegheny and Monongahela rivers flow together. And there are other rivers—the Missouri, Arkansas, Illinois, and Tennessee among them—that are sturdy branches on this huge navigational tree. Together these are called the "Western Rivers," a term coined nearly two centuries ago, when the Mississippi was the western frontier.

Steamboating on the Mississippi dates back to 1811 and the

◀ *Spray flies from the churning "bucket boards" of the* Delta Queen's *stern wheel.*

This replica of the New Orleans, *above, was built in 1911 for the boat's centennial. The* Delta Queen, *below right, carries on the tradition begun by the original* New Orleans.

pioneering *New Orleans*. This little side-wheel steamer was just 116 feet long. The finest boat—not quite the biggest, which was the *Grand Republic*—that ever served the Mississippi is generally acknowledged to be the *J. M. White*, 320 feet long and opulent in all ways, with stained-glass windows, elegant woods, crystal chandeliers, and intricate "gingerbread" wood trim. Though the steamboat was excessively ornate by modern standards, when launched in 1878 it reflected perfectly the Victorian era's taste for elegance.

In September 1811, the far more modest *New Orleans* had begun its journey downriver from Pittsburgh to its namesake city. Barely had it left the Ohio River for the Mississippi when it encountered the widespread devastation of the New Madrid, Missouri, earthquakes, the largest ever recorded in America. This series of earthquakes dramatically rearranged the landscape, forming new lakes and altering the course of the

Mississippi. Partly because of the quakes, the *New Orleans* didn't complete its trip until January, when it became the first steamboat ever to travel the lengths of the Ohio and Lower Mississippi. Western Rivers steamboats led a perilous existence, however, navigating among snags and shoals in an ever-shifting river. In 1814 *New Orleans* hit a stump and sank.

But before long, newer, bigger boats would have made the little *New Orleans* obsolete, anyway. Steamboating flourished on the Mississippi and its tributaries for much of the nineteenth century, with the Civil War causing a temporary setback. In 1834, there were 230 steam packets on the rivers. By 1849, this number had swelled to about 1,000.

The Mississippi River packets had a distinctive look, with two towering fluted smokestacks. They were built tall so

sparks spewing from the stacks would be less likely to land on the easily ignited wooden superstructures or the flammable bales of cotton typically piled on freight decks, and also to provide better draft to fan the fires in the fireboxes. A square pilothouse was generally placed in the middle of the boat, well back from the bow, where it was found on most other boats. Many of the staterooms, patronized by the well-to-do, opened onto promenade decks that swept around the vessel. Paddle wheels were better than propellers for navigating in the shallow and snag-infested rivers, so they were most common. In time, stern-wheelers came to outnumber side-wheelers.

The Delta Queen Steams On

Today, an amazing survivor, the *Delta Queen*, still paddles the Western Rivers. This steamer, which began life in 1927 in California as an overnight boat shuttling between San Francisco and Sacramento, has served the Mississippi and its tributaries since World War II. To get to the Midwest, the boat, which had been purchased by Captain Tom Greene of the family-owned Greene Lines, had to be towed 5,378 miles, including passage through the Panama Canal.

Always common to circuses and carnivals, the steam calliope (left) is now a tradition on Mississippi River steamboats. Hands on the primitive keyboard send steam roaring festively through the whistles above. Another steamboating tradition is the grand staircase (above), like this one on the Delta Queen.

With his right hand on the throttle, the Delta Queen's *chief engineer prepares to acknowledge a "slow ahead" command rung down from the bridge.*

With the bright red "bucket boards" (or paddles) of its stern wheel churning, her throaty steamboat whistle moaning, and her calliope playing, the *Delta Queen* is a remarkable link with the past. In the engine room, which passengers are welcome to visit, two cross-compound condensing steam engines generating 2,000 horsepower churn away to spin a paddle wheel 28 feet in diameter. (Most steamboats have compound engines, which use steam twice, in two cylinders. The first, high-pressure cylinder is smaller; the second, which reuses the steam after it has lost some of its pressure, is larger. "Cross-compound" means that the cylinders are side by side, rather than one following the other. "Condensing" means that exhaust steam is captured, cooled to liquid state, and reused.)

The *Delta Queen* has led something of a charmed life. The greatest threat to her existence came with the passage in 1966 of the Safety of Life at Sea law, which made the ship's wooden superstructure illegal. Recognizing that the law was written with offshore vessels in mind and that the *Delta Queen* never would be more than a few hundred feet from a riverbank, the U.S. Congress has granted the boat a series of exemptions, and the threat appears to have ended years ago.

Meanwhile, partly as a backup for the *Delta Queen,* the

Mark Twain, Steamboat Pilot

Samuel Langhorne Clemens, one of America's greatest writers, is tightly linked to the Mississippi and steamboats. He was born in Florida, Missouri, in 1835 and grew up in nearby Hannibal, a Mississippi River town where steamboats regularly stopped. Even the pen name by which he is generally known—Mark Twain—has a steamboating origin, dating from his early years as a river pilot. This was a calling then as admired by young boys as railroad engineer would be for the next generation and astronaut is today. Clemens loved the river and aspired to work on it.

When he was twenty-one, Clemens met Horace Bixby, a Mississippi River pilot, and convinced Bixby to take him on as an apprentice. Two years later he was a licensed pilot, a king of the river, guiding the majestic, tall-stacked steamboats—his childhood dream. Unhappily, this career was truncated barely two years later when the Civil War caused the suspension of civilian river traffic on the Mississippi. But by this time, Clemens had found the inspiration for his pen name, which he would adopt a few years later when working as a newspaperman in the silver-mining country of Nevada.

Since the Mississippi is a shallow river for much of its length, running aground has been a concern since the earliest days of steamboating. In an era long before such electronic devices as sonar, water depth was checked by a leadsman who stood in the boat's bow and flung a rope weighted with a lead-filled pipe into the water. The leadsman noted the "mark" on the rope when the pipe touched bottom and "sang the mark" to the wheelhouse. The second mark on the rope, or "mark twain," indicated water 2 fathoms (12 feet) deep, enough for safe passage.

Mark Twain recounted his years as a steamboat pilot in *Life on the Mississippi*, a combination of memoir and travel book. His two most famous novels, *The Adventures of Tom Sawyer* and *The Adventures of Huckleberry Finn*, are set in a river town modeled on Hannibal. Much of the latter book takes place on a raft, as Huck and Jim, an escaped slave, float south on the Mississippi, a "monstrous big river," in Huck's words, but one where you could "feel mighty free and easy and comfortable."

The Mississippi Queen*'s landing stage reaches to the levee at "Natchez Under the Hill," as the riverside area of this Mississippi city, rich with Civil War history, is known.*

Greene Lines (by then the Delta Queen Steamboat Company, which in 2006 became part of the Majestic American Line) in 1975 launched the *Mississippi Queen*, an authentic paddle-wheel (but all-steel) steamboat. Twenty years later it added the opulent *American Queen*, modeled on the *J. M. White*.

"A race between two notoriously fleet steamers was an event of vast importance," Mark Twain wrote in his book *Life on the Mississippi*, and this tradition lives on. Perhaps the most famous race of all occurred in 1870 and pitted the *Rob't E. Lee* against the *Natchez*. The *Rob't E. Lee*, remembered in song and generally acknowledged as fastest ever, easily won that New Orleans–St. Louis race with a time of 3 days, 18 hours, and 14 minutes, despite an hours-long delay caused by a burst steam pipe.

Today, fleetmates *Delta Queen* and *Mississippi Queen* race for the "golden antlers," the traditional symbol of victory that is carried proudly atop the victorious boat's pilothouse. The *Delta Queen* also races the historic day-excursion steamer *Belle of Louisville*.

By the beginning of the twentieth century, railroads had gone a long way toward replacing steamboats as the main mode of transport in mid-America. But even today, at the beginning of the twenty-first century, the *Delta Queen* and her sisters still steam along the Western Rivers.

"Choking a Stump"

The Mississippi riverboat has been unique in its ability to tie up virtually anywhere, just nuzzling up to the bank or sloping levee at a diagonal and lowering to shore a long, bridgelike "landing stage" suspended from a boom. While most boats and ships dock, on the Mississippi they land. This is as true for the huge tows that ply the Western Rivers today as it was for the grand steamboats of Mark Twain's era. ("Tows" are lash-ups of barges pushed—not pulled, as the name would suggest—by powerful towboats, today powered by diesel engine.)

To tie up once the boat lands, the crew "chokes a stump," as it's called on the river. This simply means securing a mooring line to a convenient stump or tree.

However universal this practice, it can occasionally get a captain in trouble. In June 1995, the *American Queen* was headed up the Ohio River on a shakedown (or trial) voyage just before entering regular service. Running a bit ahead of schedule, the boat tied up briefly overnight to be properly positioned for a morning photo session. When a dam release caused a five-foot drop in the river level, the *American Queen* found herself stuck fast in the Kentucky mud.

All day long a pair of powerful towboats, drafted from pushing tows loaded with coal and chemicals, tugged at the steamboat, but to no avail. Stuck she remained. Eventually, passengers were taken off, water storage tanks were drained, and the fuel was pumped onto a barge to lighten the load. Then the *American Queen* steamed off upriver, intact except for her pride.

Passengers aboard the Delta Queen *wave as the* American Queen *steams by.*

Three

Excursion Steamers
for Day-Trippers

DAY-EXCURSION STEAMERS, MANY OF THEM PROPELLED by paddle wheels, once plied most of the significant lakes and rivers of the world. They thrived in the United States but, sadly, have now vanished. However, they are still common in Europe. Seventeen classic paddle steamers continue to serve five of Switzerland's lakes each summer. Stockholm's harbor teems with excursion steamers, and they can also be found in Great Britain and in Norway, Germany, Italy, and elsewhere on the Continent.

Although these boats are historic, and some have undergone expensive restorations, they remain utilitarian as well. On Switzerland's Lake Luzern, five paddle-wheel steamers link dozens of villages with the city of Luzern. The oldest steamer, *Uri*, dates from 1901. The newest boat, the *Stadt Luzern*, was built in 1928.

On Lake Geneva, there are eight paddle steamers, five currently active. Over the years, four boats were modernized by conversion to diesel power. Testimony to Europeans' reverence for history and authenticity was a program to restore all of them to steam propulsion— though it's now suspended, with one conversion completed.

◀ *On Lake Luzern, the* Gallia *steams into Rütli, noted in legend as the site where a united Switzerland was formed.*

*Paddles churning,
the Lake Luzern steamer* Uri
leaves Treib.

The Lake Luzern and Lake Geneva boats, as well as those serving other Swiss lakes—Zürich, Brienz, Thun—are all side-wheelers and similar in design. They are long, low, and graceful, with a single tall, raked stack behind the wheelhouse, which sits forward atop the second of two decks. This second deck is typically reserved for travelers with first-class tickets—a class distinction also maintained on most European trains though unusual in North America. The main deck generally holds a dining saloon—often ornate, with carved wood and etched glass. Meals are served in the style you'd expect in a good restaurant. Many of the boats are quite elegant and feature gilded ornamentation on the bow and paddle boxes.

A nearly universal feature of excursion boats in Switzerland and elsewhere is an open engine room, visible to passengers. Leaning on a railing, adults and children alike look down at the plunging connecting rods and whirling crankshaft. They watch the agile oiler—the engine-room helper—dart his hand into the dancing machinery to turn down the handles on the lubricators. They see the engineer adjust the throttle in response to instructions rung down from the wheelhouse. The surging, churning engine slows gradually, then settles to a stop. The engineer waits for the telegraph to ring and its arrow to swing to "slow ahead" before setting the massive, shiny, well-oiled machinery in motion again.

Boats powered by reciprocating steam move in serene silence, lacking the vibration and rumble of diesel-powered vessels. They're so quiet that the trilling bell of the telegraph can be heard up on deck. Aboard paddle steamers, passengers can hear the slosh of the paddles pushing water as the captain calls for "full astern" when approaching a dock and the wheels churn vigorously in reverse to slow the boat.

The Steamboats of Scandinavia

Walk along the streets that line the old harbor of Stockholm, Sweden, and you'll see a different breed of steamboat. Propeller-driven, they are chunkier than the Swiss boats, but graceful in their own way, with the tall stacks characteristic of steamboats (as opposed to the stubbier stacks that work for diesel boats).

Stockholm's archipelago, or group of islands, extends far into the Baltic Sea and numbers an astonishing twenty-four thousand. Many years ago, hundreds of steamboats sailed among them and were the only means of transport. Though roads and bridges have made them less essential, steamboats are as much fun as ever, and many survive. Some, like the *Blidösund* (built in 1911 and among the last remaining coal-fired Stockholm boats), have been restored and are operated by enthusiasts. Others still steam for their traditional owners.

Not far away, in Norway, the world's oldest paddle steamer in scheduled service sails on Lake Mjøsa. The *Skibladner*, which locals call the White Swan, was built in 1856. As the steamer glides gracefully across the lake, its tall smokestack is reminiscent of a swan's proud neck. Its white paint furthers

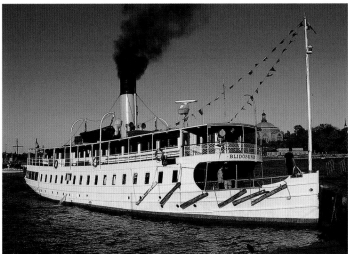

In Stockholm Harbor, coal-burning Blidösund *smokes it up.*

Lunch is served aboard the Waxholm.

Propellers Versus Paddle Wheels

In 1848, the British Admiralty pitted the propeller-driven HMS *Rattler* against the paddle-wheeler *Alecto* to see which of the two kinds of steam propulsion was better. Although the *Rattler* won, the debate was far from settled. Though propellers almost immediately replaced paddle wheels on oceangoing vessels, paddle-wheel technology lingered on aboard lake and river steamboats that were built up to a century after the Admiralty's epic contest.

Why did the paddle wheel last so long, since propellers are more efficient? For one thing, paddle wheels are better in low-water conditions, since propellers require deeper water and are more easily damaged should the boat run aground. Paddle wheels also make a boat easier to maneuver. They can be reversed quickly for faster stopping. In many instances, the two wheels of a side-wheeler are powered and controlled independently, a great help in coming alongside a pier. Since lake and river steamers make frequent calls at docks in shallow harbors, paddle wheels can be a double benefit.

Since that's the case, why did stern-wheelers become dominant on the Mississippi and its tributaries? In time that river system was developed with dams and locks for heavy-duty commercial traffic, and the narrower stern-wheelers (without the bulge of side wheels) could more readily fit into those locks. Also, a stern-wheel towboat could lash barges to its side, while a side-wheeler obviously couldn't.

Of course, diesel propulsion is more efficient than either screw-driven or paddle-wheel-driven steam, both of which are labor-intensive.

As the Waverley's *builder's plate makes clear, side-wheel paddle steamers were launched into the middle of the twentieth century. Still steaming in preservation, the* Waverley *sails the shores and islands of Great Britain. Side-wheelers' often ornate paddle boxes contain the spray from the wheels.*

that illusion, as does the bulge of its paddle boxes, much like a swimming swan's folded wings.

For a full century and a half, *Skibladner* has sailed the length of Mjøsa, the country's largest lake, for the Opland Steamship Company. Today's passengers are aboard more for pleasure than transportation—trains offer a far faster trip between the same points—but otherwise the boat's mission and mode of operations are unchanged. Symbolic of the elegance of an earlier period is all the brass visible on deck: wheel, binnacle (housing the compass), bell, running lights, knobs lining the bridge-deck railing, and four brass cannons (ceremonial, not warlike). Today they gleam as bright with polish as they no doubt did one hundred fifty years ago.

North American Steam Survivors

The last regularly scheduled excursion steamboats to operate in the United States outside of a museum were the Bob-Lo boats, the *Columbia* and *Ste. Claire*. For the better part of a century, these boats shuttled Detroiters to the amusement park on Bob-Lo Island, where children and adults alike could enjoy many rides, including a miniature railway. There was picnicking, and dancing in the pavilion. The boats were retired in 1991, and the park closed two years later.

At the Mystic Seaport Museum of America and the Sea in Connecticut, the tiny (just 57 feet long), coal-fired *Sabino* putters along the Mystic River and makes longer cruises into Long Island Sound. This little gem was built in Maine, where it originally served.

In Ontario's Muskoka Lakes Region, a popular resort area, the tall-stacked, coal-burning RMS *Segwun* (built in 1887

as the *Nipissing*, rebuilt as a propeller boat in 1925, and restored to service in 1981 after a twenty-year lay-up) still steams. ("RMS" means Royal Mail Ship, a designation stemming from Canada's remaining ties to the British Crown.) The *Segwun* proved so popular that its operator, the Muskoka Lakes Navigation and Hotel Company, built a sister boat in 2002. The *Wenonah II* is larger and has modern amenities such as air conditioning and an elevator, but its profile copies the *Segwun*'s.

Two very different North American excursion steamers are the Segwun *(top) and* Columbia.

Four

Ferryboats,
Workhorses of the Water

OVER THE CENTURIES, FERRYBOATS HAVE PROVIDED the missing link in land transportation, bridging a water gap where no actual bridge existed. Typically this gap was a river, though it could also be a sound separating an offshore island from the mainland, or sometimes even a lake so big that looping around it would be too time-consuming. Often humble, ferryboats provide an important service, shuttling pedestrians and vehicles. As bridges and tunnels have been built over the years, many ferries have become obsolete. However, many others are still busy and essential today. These include New York City's famous Staten Island Ferry and the boats of Istanbul's Bosporus Strait. And any long-standing ferry service certainly has steamboats somewhere in its history.

The orange boats of the Staten Island Ferry sail across Upper New York Bay to link downtown Manhattan, called the Battery, with Staten Island, one of New York City's five boroughs. The last steamboats in the fleet were retired in 1982. In 2005, three new boats

◀ *The* Martha's Vineyard *sails from Bridgeport, Connecticut, bound across Long Island Sound for Port Jefferson on Long Island.*

arrived, effectively replacing the first diesel boats, a trio from 1965. Operated by the city since 1905, today's boats carry 19 million riders annually. This ferry system has always been a good buy, but since 1997 it has had the most reasonable fare possible: It's free.

The Boats of Puget Sound

Located on Puget Sound, Seattle is another city that relies heavily on a busy fleet of ferries. With ten routes, twenty terminals, and twenty-eight boats, Washington State Ferries boasts the most extensive network in the country. The company's steamboat era ended in 1987, when the then sixty-year-old *Nisqually* was converted to diesel power.

One traditional steamboat, the *Virginia V*, from Puget Sound's famed Mosquito Fleet of ferries, remains. So many of these little ferries once buzzed about the sound, shuttling passengers and freight, that they were said to be "thick as mosquitoes." A survivor with a wooden hull and century-old engine, the *Virginia V* still steams today, though only in charter and occasional excursion service.

Another active ferry service links the parks and gardens of Toronto Island with downtown. Though the current fleet is diesel-powered, the ferry *Trillium*, a paddle steamer, has been lovingly restored and now sails for groups in charter service.

Virginia V's *captain.*

The Nisqually *as a steam ferry.*

Side-wheel steam ferry Trillium.

Coastal Ferries, Cut from a Different Cloth

Among the last-surviving of the traditional steam-powered coastal ferries was the *Martha's Vineyard*, built in 1923 to carry passengers and automobiles between the islands of Nantucket and Martha's Vineyard and the Massachusetts mainland at Woods Hole and New Bedford. This handsome vessel, with greater freeboard (the distance from waterline to deck) than lake steamers (since coastal boats were subject to higher seas), was eventually converted to diesel and spent its last working days shuttling across Long Island Sound from Bridgeport, Connecticut, to Port Jefferson, on Long Island. For three decades a preservation group worked to save the *Martha's Vineyard* or sister *Nobska*, but to no avail. The routes across Nantucket Sound remain busy today, but the last steam-powered vessel to work there, the *Naushon*, was retired in the 1980s.

Thousands of ferries still ply the waters of the world, and they come in all sizes and shapes. However, the Millersburg Ferry must be among the most unusual. *Roaring Bull* and *Falcon* paddle across the wide Susquehanna River in central Pennsylvania. The river is so shallow—as low as two feet in some places—that only this type of ferry would work: a rough-hewn, boxy wooden vessel with flats (or barges) lashed alongside to carry automobiles. Though *Roaring Bull*'s wheels are now driven by a gasoline-powered flathead V-8 engine from a 1949 Ford truck, the steam-powered, side-wheel *Enterprise* of 1873 was the first paddle-wheeler to serve the Millersburg Ferry. Before that, boats were poled across.

Ferries link opposite sides of rivers or offshore islands with the mainland. Some, like the boats of the Alaska Marine Highway, make multiple-day voyages and link countries. At least one ferry serves two continents: the Istanbul boats that cross the Bosporus, shuttling between Europe and Asia.

The Naushon *was the last steamboat to serve Nantucket and Martha's Vineyard.*

■ *31*

Five

Bulk Carriers Serve
the Great Lakes

THE LAKERS ARE A PECULIAR AND PARTICULAR BREED, odd in appearance, with a shape determined by their sole role: moving bulk commodities such as iron ore, grain, coal, limestone, and cement. All lakers were once powered by steam, and boats with steam-turbine plants have survived into the twenty-first century, though fewer and fewer remain.

The classic "laker" look, which lasted into the 1960s and was exemplified by the *S. T. Crapo*, originated almost exactly a century earlier. That design created two separate worlds afloat. The wheelhouse and quarters for the captain, mates, wheelsmen, and deck crew were forward; the engine room and quarters for the chief and assistant engineers, engine-room crew, stewards, and cooks, along with galley

◀ *With a feather of steam at its stack, turbine-powered* Middletown, *built in 1942, loads at the Duluth, Missabe & Iron Range Railroad's massive ore dock in Duluth, Minnesota.*

■ *33*

and dining rooms, were aft. This placed navigation forward for better visibility, and the mechanical department aft, where the engines had to be.

The center of the vessel, accounting for most of its length, was an unbroken series of holds, easily accessible for swift loading and unloading. These holds were secured for safety under way with watertight hatch covers. Lakers have flat, straight sides to enable them to fit through the locks that are central to Great Lakes shipping.

The Soo Locks at Sault Ste. Marie, where Michigan and Ontario meet, allow ships to negotiate the 12-foot drop from Lake Superior into Lake Huron. (Locks are chambers that can be flooded with or drained of water; thus a ship can be carried to a higher or lower level than the one at which it entered.)

Canada Steamship Line's SCL Tadoussac, *a diesel-powered self-unloader, passes "upbound" (away from the Atlantic Ocean) through the Welland Canal.*

Unloading taconite pellets—low-grade iron ore crushed and reconstituted as marblelike balls—at a steel mill in Hamilton, Ontario.

Enter the Steam Turbine

The steam turbine literally burst upon the maritime scene in 1897 when the 100-foot-long yacht *Turbina* sped uninvited among the ships assembled for the Spithead Review of the Royal Navy, held at Portsmouth, England. The occasion was Queen Victoria's Diamond Jubilee, so the Prince of Wales and many other dignitaries were on hand. They could hardly fail to be impressed when the little steam-turbine-powered vessel, designed by Irish engineer Sir Charles Algernon Parsons, easily outran the patrol boats (powered by reciprocating steam engines) that tried to catch it.

Turbina could make speeds up to 34 knots (about 30 miles per hour), and before many years passed, steam turbines began to supplant reciprocating steam engines in most types of vessels. In a turbine engine, pressurized steam spins rotors, converting thermal energy to mechanical. Its advantages over a reciprocating engine include providing more power with less weight (always a major consideration aboard boats). Also, the spinning turbine generates a rotary motion, ideal for driving a propeller, while the power of an up-and-down reciprocating engine must be converted by linkage to turn a propeller or paddle wheel.

On the Great Lakes, turbines eventually supplanted reciprocating steamers, but not until the 1960s. They in turn have been largely replaced by boats with diesel engines—a technology that entered the maritime world in the teens and became dominant in the last third of the twentieth century.

Steam turbine Mapleglen *passes upbound through the Welland Canal's Lock 3.*

Two of the five parallel locks are now in service, including the Poe Lock, which can accommodate the 1,000-foot-long "superlakers" that were introduced in 1971, two years after Poe opened. However, these boats are landlocked, since they are too long to pass through the 27-mile-long Welland Canal, which lifts boats up the Niagara Escarpment, allowing them to pass from Lake Ontario into Lake Erie. The same geographic feature that created Niagara Falls requires this dramatic rise.

The canal can accommodate vessels that are up to 736 feet long. For many years after the current Welland Canal (there were three earlier ones) was opened in 1932, that effectively limited vessel size. But since the "1,000-footers" are largely dedicated to hauling iron ore to the mills on Lakes Erie and Michigan, their entrapment on the upper lakes is not a problem.

The current Great Lakes fleet numbers in the hundreds, owned more or less evenly by Canadian and American companies. In addition, many oceangoing ships, called "salties," enter the lakes from around the world. Another major innovation that changed the look of lakers was the development of self-unloaders—boats with a somewhat ungainly above-deck apparatus containing a conveyor belt that can be boomed out to shore. This allows lakers to unload bulk cargoes themselves, easily and anywhere. (Vessels without self-unloaders are now called "straight-deckers.")

Despite changes in style and powering, the traditional steam-powered bulk carrier is still a presence on the Great Lakes. The oldest vessel is the *St. Mary's Challenger*, a cement boat built in 1906 and still powered by a reciprocating steam engine, though a sophisticated version. Dozens of bulk carriers still have steam turbines whirring in their engine rooms.

A steam turbine when launched in 1960, the Comeaudoc was dieselized at age twenty-five. Typical of "straight-deckers," it uses a gantry that rolls the length of the vessel to lift hatch covers.

The Sinking of the Edmund Fitzgerald

On November 10, 1975, the ore boat *Edmund Fitzgerald* sank during a treacherous fall storm. All twenty-nine crewmen were lost when the vessel plunged suddenly to the bottom of Lake Superior, making it the most famous lake boat (much as the ill-fated *Titanic* is the most famous ocean liner).

Until that moment, the "*Fitz*," a 729-foot-long straight-decker built in 1958 and powered with steam turbines, was just another Great Lakes bulk carrier. It was one of the iron boats that carried ore from the mines west of Lake Superior to eastern mills. When it sank, the *Fitzgerald* was bound from Superior, Wisconsin, to Detroit, Michigan, laden with taconite pellets (balls of processed ore) and under the command of Captain Ernest McSorley.

Along the way, the *Fitzgerald* encountered winds gusting to 95 miles per hour, which whipped up swells 30 feet high. After "checking down" (slowing speed, in Great Lakes maritime talk), the *Fitzgerald* was caught by the slower *Arthur M. Anderson*, a similar vessel, under the command of Jesse "Bernie" Cooper. The two captains would radio back and forth in the hours ahead, and Cooper would follow the "*Fitz*" on his radar screen.

Then, at 7:25 p.m., the *Edmund Fitzgerald* simply vanished from the *Anderson*'s screen. The doomed boat was a mere 17 miles from the safety of Whitefish Bay.

The reason for the *Fitzgerald*'s abrupt sinking is still in question, though the probable cause, eventually accepted by U.S. Coast Guard investigators, was that the hatch covers sprung leaks, allowing the holds to flood. Other possibilities are that the boat hit a shoal or simply broke in two in the storm—which, before radio contact was lost, McSorley called the worst he'd ever seen.

Though big news at the time, the *Fitzgerald*'s sinking probably would have slipped from public consciousness had not Canadian composer and folksinger Gordon Lightfoot written "The Wreck of the *Edmund Fitzgerald*," a haunting ballad about how "That good ship and true was a bone to be chewed/When the gales of November came early."

Six

Trains Across the Water

HERE AND THERE AROUND THE WORLD, BODIES OF WATER interrupted rail routes, and railroad car ferries were required to supply the missing link. Steam-powered railroad car ferries did bridge some North American rivers, most notably the Detroit, and many freight cars were barged across the Hudson River by steam-powered tugboats. But America's most notable and longest-lasting railroad car ferries crossed Lake Michigan, linking Michigan and Wisconsin, and the Straits of Mackinac, linking Michigan's Upper and Lower Peninsulas. The ferries that crossed the straits were especially important before 1976, when a soaring suspension bridge did that far more efficiently.

The most remarkable survivor of all the railroad car ferries was the *Chief Wawatam*, which shuttled across the straits from 1911 until

◄ *With its bow sea gate up, the* Chief Wawatam *arrives at Mackinaw City on Michigan's Lower Peninsula.*

C&O car ferry Spartan—*exact sister to the* Badger, *which still operates—steams into Manitowoc, Wisconsin, at dawn.*

retirement in 1984. With its wooden pilothouse, tall twin stacks, and bow sea gate that opened wide like a whale's mouth, it was a curious but memorable vessel. Like all railroad car ferries, it was flat as a board, since the tracks had to be perfectly level. Missing was the graceful sheer, the curving upsweep at both ends, that once characterized hull shapes. Right to the end, the vessel was coal fired, with no mechanical stokers—a so-called "hand-bomber," meaning that the crew had to shovel the coal into the fireboxes.

Sometimes passenger trains as well as freight trains rode railroad car ferries, and until 1955 the *Chief* carried the coaches of the *Lake Superior Limited*. (In Europe, passenger-train ferry services across the Strait of Messina in Italy and across the Baltic Sea from Malmö, Sweden, to Berlin, Germany, survived into the twenty-first century.)

The Lake Michigan ferries provided a way for freight cars to avoid the long, expensive, time-consuming detour around the lake's southern end. The first ferries, operated by

Clockwise from top left: Working on the Lake Michigan railroad car ferries: a fire-man checks the fire in the Badger's stokehold; the wheelsman and captain peer into the fog from the Viking's wheelhouse; a deckhand winds up to fling ashore the light "throwing line," attached to the steel cables that the boat will use to winch itself into its slip.

the Toledo, Ann Arbor & Northern Michigan Railroad, began steaming in 1892 between Frankfort, Michigan, and Kewaunee, Wisconsin. The Pere Marquette, which later became part of the Chesapeake & Ohio Railway, also operated a fleet of cross-lake boats, as did the Grand Trunk.

All these boats were built as steamers, though a few were converted to diesel power before retirement. They had aft sea gates, which raised so switch engines could push railroad cars aboard onto the four tracks that were standard. Once in place, the cars were lashed down with chains, and wheel stops were clamped onto the rails to keep cars secure should the boats hit heavy seas. The boats carried automobiles as well as train cars, and the Pere Marquette vessels also had many staterooms and a comfortable lounge and restaurant. But business dwindled, and

42 ∎ *Docked at Lake Betsie in Frankfort, Michigan, Ann Arbor's* Arthur K. Atkinson *(at left) has been dieselized, but the* City of Milwaukee *shows that it's very much in steam.*

by the 1970s the Lake Michigan boats were clearly in decline. Two of the former C&O boats struggled on under different ownership until 1990, but they shut down, and that was the end.

Though not quite, really. One of the boats, the *Badger*—built in 1952, coal fired, with a sophisticated Skinner Uniflow reciprocating engine—was purchased and reentered service in 1992. With its railroad tracks paved over, the boat carries cars, trucks, and people between Ludington, Michigan, and Manitowoc, Wisconsin, only during the summer.

Europe gave up on floating passenger trains more grudgingly than America did. The sleeping-cars-only *Night Ferry* between London and Paris lasted until 1980 and was among the most glamorous.

Even today, passenger trains from the Italian mainland en route to Sicily cross the Strait of Messina by ferry. Railway coaches make the thirty-five-minute journey from Villa San Giovanni on the mainland to Messina by boat. Metal squeals and shrieks as the coaches are pushed or pulled over the loading apron. Here the time-honored ritual of passengers riding a train and a ship at the same time lives on.

Train ferries shuttle back and forth across the Strait of Messina off the coast of Italy.

Seven

Keeping Steam Up

THOUGH MORE THAN HALF A CENTURY HAS PASSED since steamboats were in their heyday, a surprising number remain active. Most are not strictly museum pieces, since they provide transportation. Still, few or none of them would have survived were steamboats not inherently historic—and fun.

In fact, steamboats have proved so attractive that some new ones actually were built in the latter part of the twentieth century. *Mississippi Queen* and *American Queen* are examples, though the *American Queen*'s steam-powered paddle wheel gets help from diesel-electric propellers. Sharing the lower Mississippi with these boats is the *Natchez*, a day-excursion steamer sailing out of New Orleans. This boat, a classic Western Rivers stern-wheeler in appearance with tall stacks and centered wheelhouse, was built in 1975 and is all-steel (a Coast Guard requirement for new boats). Its engine came from an old towboat.

◄ *The* Lac du Saint Sacrament *on Lake George, New York.*

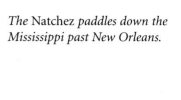

The Natchez *paddles down the Mississippi past New Orleans.*

Similar in its Mississippi styling, the *Minne-ha-ha* seems somewhat out of place on New York State's Lake George, where it has steamed in excursion service since it was built in 1969. Lake George had its own fleet of classic excursion steamers, as did larger Lake Champlain, just to the north. One of the Champlain Transportation Company's boats, the *Ticonderoga*, has been preserved—but high and dry, two miles from the lake, at Vermont's Shelburne Museum.

Straying even further from authenticity, other modern boats have been built to look like steamboats but have diesel propulsion. Imitation Western Rivers boats sailing on the Columbia River are the *Queen of the West* and *Empress of the North*, now part of the Majestic America Line. Inspired by the look of Northeastern coastal overnight boats, the *Pilgrim Belle* was built for those waters but now sails in Alaska as the *Spirit of '98*.

The Lake George Steamboat Company, which operates the *Minne-ha-ha*, in 1989 launched, largely for dinner cruises, the *Lac du Saint Sacrament*, diesel-powered and modeled on the 1920s Hudson River steamer *Peter Stuyvesant*. Also in the fleet is the *Mohican*, built in 1906 as a steamboat but dieselized and much modified since. Which of the three is the most authentic?

So steamboats live on—here and there in North America, far more commonly in Europe. Stern-wheel, side-wheel, or driven by propellers, they march up and down rivers, circle lakes, and steam to offshore islands. A few haul cargo, but most carry people. For those fortunate passengers, these steamboats are a feast for the senses: a cooling breeze, the sound of a throaty whistle and the slosh of a paddle or hull through water, the smell of steam and hot lubricating oil, and the blue of water all around.

Author's Note

The best way to understand a steamboat is to actually climb aboard one, and that's possible in surprisingly many places across North America and around the world. Following is a list of Web sites (active at date of publication) for more information on many of the surviving steamboats and other vessels discussed in this book.

Alaska Marine Highway www.akferry.org

American Queen, *Delta Queen*, *Empress of the North*, *Mississippi Queen*, and *Queen of the West* www.majesticamericanline.com

Badger www.ssbadger.com

Belle of Louisville www.belleoflouisville.org

Columbia and *Ste. Claire* www.bobloboat.com

Lac du Saint Sacrament, *Minne-ha-ha*, and *Mohican* www.lakegeorgesteamboat.com

Millersburg Ferry www.millersburg.com/attractions/ferry.html

Natchez www.steamboatnatchez.com

Sabino www.mysticseaport.org

Segwun and *Wenonah II* www.segwun.com

Skibladner www.skibladner.no/engelsk/

Staten Island Ferry www.siferry.com

Swiss (and Italian) paddle steamers www.swissitalianpaddlesteamers.com

Ticonderoga www.shelburnemuseum.org

Virginia V www.virginiav.org

Washington State Ferries www.wsdot.wa.gov/ferries

Glossary

Aftercabin: Structure (particularly common on lake boats) at the rear of a vessel that houses the quarters for the engine crew as well as galley and mess.

Binnacle: A case holding, and protecting, a boat's compass.

Bow: The front of a boat.

Bucket boards: Wooden blades, or paddles, of a paddle wheel that dip into the water and propel the boat.

Bulk carrier: The typical freight carrier on the Great Lakes with a series of holds for such dry cargoes as grain, coal, gravel, or cement. Bulk carriers of liquid cargoes are called tankers.

Choke a stump: To tie up along a riverbank by using an available tree or stump.

Compound engine: An engine that uses steam twice, in two cylinders—a smaller, high-pressure cylinder and a second, larger cylinder that reuses the steam after it has lost some of its pressure.

Condensing engine: An engine that captures exhaust steam, cools it to liquid state, and then reuses the water.

Connecting rods: In an engine, the linkage between piston and crankshaft.

Crankshaft: The part of a reciprocating steam engine that converts the linear motion of pistons to the rotary motion needed to drive a propeller or paddle wheel.

Freeboard: The height of the hull from waterline to deck.

Laker or lake boat: A vessel designed to carry bulk commodities on the Great Lakes.

Landing stage: A long, heavy bridgelike ramp lowered to shore by boom over which passengers leave or enter a vessel.

Leadsman: Crew member who checked river depth with a lead line.

Packet: A boat that carried freight, passengers, and mail and operated on a set schedule.

Paddle box: Structure that encloses a paddle wheel to minimize spray. Though nearly all side-wheelers had them, few stern-wheelers did.

Reciprocating engine: The slang term "up-and-downer" is descriptive, since in this type of steam engine, pistons move in and out of vertical cylinders to generate power.

Sea Gate: On an automobile or railroad car ferry, a section of the hull, either bow or stern, that raises to let vehicles in or out.

Self-unloader: A boat that carries its own crane and conveyor for unloading cargo.

Side-wheel steamer or side-wheeler: A boat with two paddle wheels, one on each side of the hull.

Steam turbine: An engine using pressurized steam to turn rotors and thus generate power.

Stern: The rear or aft end of a boat.

Stern-wheel steamer or stern-wheeler: A boat with a single large paddle wheel at the stern.

Stokehold: Room for the steam boilers, fireboxes, and coal bunkers.

Straight-decker: A Great Lakes bulk carrier without self-unloading gear; seen from the side, the unencumbered hatch covers present a "straight" profile.

Telegraph: An electronic or mechanical device allowing navigating officers in the wheelhouse to communicate with officers in the engine room.

Tow: An unpowered barge or, more often, group of barges lashed together and pushed by a powered vessel called a towboat.

Western Rivers: Rivers flowing into the Gulf of Mexico, hence the Mississippi and its tributaries. The term predates navigation on the rivers of the West Coast.

Wheelhouse: Forward structure on a boat from which captain and crew navigate. On the Mississippi River and tributaries, the wheelhouse typically is in the middle of the boat and is called a pilothouse.

Index

Adventures of Huckleberry Finn, The (Twain), 19
Adventures of Tom Sawyer, The (Twain), 19
Alaska Marine Highway, *31*
Alecto, 26
Alexander Hamilton, 12
American Queen, 9, 20, 21, 45
Arthur M. Anderson, 36

Badger, 9, 43
barges, 31
   railroad car, 39
   stern-wheelers and, 26
   See also tows
Belle of Louisville, 20
Blidösund, 25
Bob-Lo Island steamers, 27
Bosporus Strait, ferries of, 29, 31
Brienz, Lake, 24

Canada
   excursion steamers of, 27
   lakers of, 37
canal boats, 11
Chesapeake & Ohio Railway, 41, 43
Chief Wawatam, 39–40
Civil War, effect on steamboating; 16, 19
Clemens, Samuel Langhorne.
   See Twain, Mark
Clermont. See North River Steam Boat of Clermont
coal
   as laker cargo, 5, 33
   as steamer fuel, 6, 8–9, 27, 40 43
Columbia, 27
Crapo. See S. T. Crapo

Delta Queen, 9, 17–20
Delta Queen Steamboat Company, 20
diesel engines, 30
   on Great Lakes, 35
   vs. reciprocating steam engines, 24
   vs. steam, 23, 24, 26, 35, 41

Edmund Fitzgerald, sinking of, 36
Empress of the North, 46
engineers, steamboats, 6, 9, 24
engine rooms
   laker, 6, 9, 33
   open to passengers, 24
engines. *See* diesel engines; reciprocating steam engines; steam turbines.
Enterprise, 31
Erie, Lake
   Lake Ontario to, 37
   superlakers on, 37
Europe, excursion steamers of, 23. *See also* France; Germany; Great Britain; Italy; Norway; Sweden; Switzerland; Turkey
excursion boats, 9, 11, 23

Falcon, 31

ferries, 29–31
   car-carrying, 31
   diesel-powered, 30, 31
   gasoline-powered, 31
   railroad car, 9, 39–43
ferryboats. *See* ferries
firemen, steamboats, 8
Fitch, John, 12
flatboats, 11
Fulton, Robert, 12, 13

Geneva, Lake, 23–24
George, Lake, 46
Germany
   excursion steamers of, 23
   passenger train ferries to, 40
Grand Republic, 16
Grand Trunk Railroad, 41
Great Britain.
   car ferries to/from, 43
   excursion steamers of, 23
Great Lakes, 6
   steamers on, 5–9, 11–12, 33–37
   See also lakers; individual lakes by name
Greene Lines, 17, 20

horses, as power source, 11
Hudson River
   steamboats on, 12, 13, 15
Hudson River Day (Night) Line, 12
Huron, Lake
   to Lake Superior, 34–37

iron ore, as lake cargo, 5, 33, 36, 37
   See also taconite
Italy
   excursion steamers of, 23
   passenger train ferries of, 40, 43

J. M. White, 16
   as *American Queen* model, 20

Lac du Saint Sacrament, 46
Lake George Steamboat Company, 46
lakers, 5–9, 33–37
   See also *S. T. Crapo*; superlakers
lakes
   Canadian, 9, 27. *See also* Great Lakes
   Norwegian, 25, 27
   Swiss, 9, 23–24
   U.S., 46. *See also* Great Lakes
Lake Superior Limited (passenger train), 40
Life on the Mississippi (Twain), 19, 20
locks, 34
   of Great Lakes, 34–37
   river, 26
Long Island Sound, ferries of, 27, 31
Luzern, Lake, 23–24

Majestic American Line, 20, 46
Martha's Vineyard, 31
Messina, Strait of, 40
Michigan, Lake
   railroad car ferries on, 38–43
   S. T. Crapo on, 5–9, 33
   superlakers on, 37
Millersville, (Pa.) Ferry, 31
Minne-ha-ha, 46
Mississippi Queen, 9, 20, 45
Mississippi River
   steamboats on, 9, 13, 15–21, 45
Mjøsa, Lake, 25, 27
Mohican, 46
Mosquito Fleet, 30
mules, as power source, 11
Muskoka Lakes, Ontario, 9, 27
Mystic (Conn.) Seaport Museum of America and Sea, 27

Natchez, 20, 45
Naushon, 31
Newcomen, Thomas, 12
New Orleans, 13, 16
Night Ferry, 43
Nobska, 31
North River Steam Boat of Clermont, 13
Norway, excursion steamers of, 23, 25, 27

Ohio River
   steamboats on, 13, 15, 16, 21
oil, as steamboat fuel, 6, 9
   See also diesel engines
oilers (engine-room workers), 24
Ontario, Lake
   to Lake Erie, 37
Opland Steamship Company, 27
ore. *See* iron ore

packets, 11
   Mississippi River, 16–17
paddles, 12, 18
paddle-wheelers, 11–13, 17
   Swiss, 9
   See also Mississippi River, steamboats on; side-wheelers; stern-wheelers
Parsons, Charles Algernon, 35
Pere Marquette Railway, 41
Peter Stuyvesant, 46
Pilgrim Belle, 46
pistons, 5, 9
propellers, 11, 25
   paddle wheels vs., 17, 26
   turbine-powered, 35
Puget Sound, ferries of, 30

Queen of the West, 46

races, steamboat, 20, 26
railroads, as steamboat competition, 12, 20, 27

See also ferries, railroad car
Rattler, HMS, 26
reciprocating steam engines, 5, 9, 35, 43
   vs. diesel, 24
   vs. steam turbines, 11–12, 35
rivers, steamboats on U. S., 9, 15–21
   See also individual rivers by name
Roaring Bull, 31
Rob't E. Lee, 20

Sabino, 27
Seattle (Wash.), ferries of, 30
Segwun, RMS, 9, 27
side-wheelers, 11, 16, 17
   vs. stern-wheelers, 26
   Swiss, 24
Skibladner, 25, 27
Soo Locks, 34, 37
Spirit of '98, 46
Stadt Luzern, 23
Staten Island Ferry, 29–30
S. T. Crapo, 5–9, 33
   retired, 9
steam
   advent of, 11–13
   as dying technology, 5
   vs. sail, 12
   sails and, 11, 13
   See also steamboats; steamships
steamboats
   demise of, 5, 12
   diesel-assisted, 45
   excursion, 20, 23–27
   first American, 12
   Hudson River, 12, 13, 15, 46
   imitation, 46
   luxurious, 16, 24, 27
   as museum pieces, 46
   propeller-driven, 11, 17, 25, 26, 35
   vs. railroads, 12, 20, 27
   See also ferries, railroad car
   in Staten Island Ferry service, 29
   and steamships contrasted, 12
   steel, 20, 45
   today, 45–46
   See also excursion boats; ferries; paddle-wheelers; reciprocating steam engines; steam turbines
steam engines
   diesel power vs., 23, 24, 26, 41
   first, 12
   See also reciprocating steam engines; steam turbines
steamships
   oceangoing, 11, 12
   and steamboats contrasted, 12
   See also packets
steam turbines, 11–12, 33, 35, 37
   vs. diesel power, 35
   vs. reciprocating steam engines, 11–12, 35

Ste. Claire, 27
stern-wheelers, 11, 17, 45
   vs. side-wheelers, 26
St. Mary's Challenger, 37
stokehold, 8
Superior, Lake
   Edmund Fitzgerald to bottom of, 36
   to Lake Huron, 34, 37
superlakers, 37
Sweden
   excursion steamers of, 23, 25
   passenger train ferries of, 40
   steamboats of, 9
Switzerland
   excursion steamers of, 23–24
   steamboats of, 9

taconite, 36
Thun, Lake, 24
telegraph, shipboard, 6, 9 , 24
Ticonderoga, 46
Titanic, 36
Toledo, Ann Arbor & Northern Michigan Railroad, 41
towboats, modern, 21, 26
tows, 21
Trillium, 30
tugboats, steam, 39
Turbina, 35
turbines. *See* steam turbines
Turkey, ferries of, 29, 31
Twain, Mark (pseudo Samuel Langhorne Clemens), 19–21

Uri, 23

Virginia V, 30

Washington State Ferries, 30
Watt, James, 12
Welland Canal, 37
Wenonah II, 27
"Wreck of the Edmund Fitzgerald, The" (Lightfoot), 6, 36

Zürich, Lake, 24

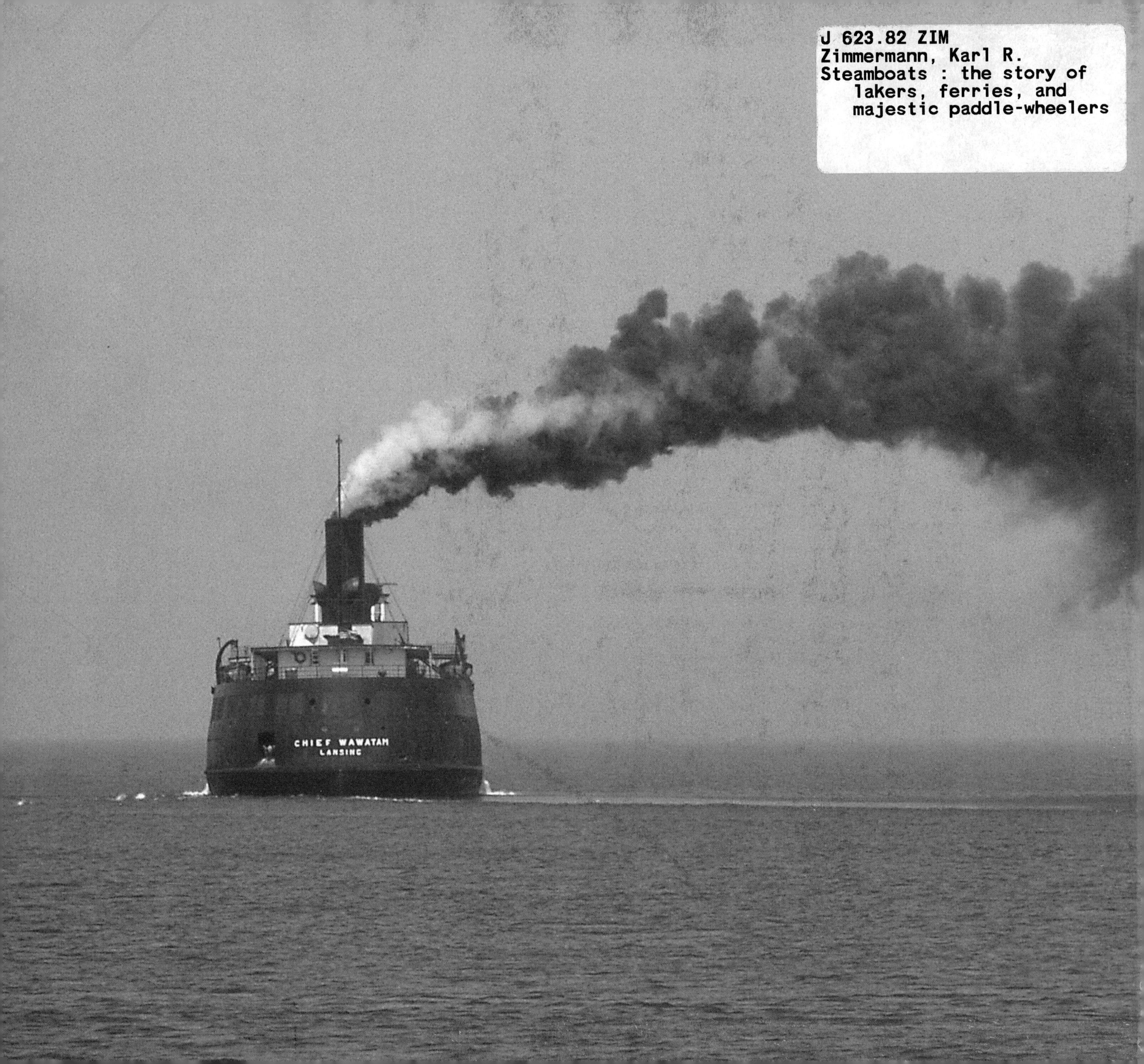
CHIEF WAWATAM
LANSING